This
Adu
The
requ

Visiting the Past

Auschwitz

Jane Shuter

Heinemann LIBRARY

First published in Great Britain by Heinemann Library,

Halley Court, Jordan Hill, Oxford OX2 8EJ,

a division of Reed Educational and Professional Publishing Ltd.

Heinemann is a registered trademark of Reed Educational & Professional Publishing Limited.

OXFORD MELBOURNE AUCKLAND

JOHANNESBURG BLANTYRE GABORONE

IBADAN PORTSMOUTH NH (USA) CHICAGO

Designed by Visual Image
Illustrations by Visual Image
Printed in Hong Kong

03 02 01 00 99
10 9 8 7 6 5 4 3 2 1

ISBN 0 431 02774 9

British Library Cataloguing in Publication Data

Shuter, Jane
  Auschwitz. – (Visiting the past)
  1. Auschwitz (Concentration camp) – Juvenile literature
  2. Holocaust, Jewish (1939–1945), – Poland – Juvenile literature
  I. Title
  940.5'317'4386
  ISBN 0431 02774 9

Acknowledgements

The Publishers would like to thank Emma Robertson and Magnet Harlequin for permission to reproduce all
photographs, apart from those on pages 7 (lower), 10 (lower) and 16, which are reproduced with
permission of the Panstwowe Muzeum Oswiecim [Auschwitz State Museum].

Cover photograph reproduced with permission of AKG London.

The Publishers would like to thank Joe Scott for his comments in the preparation of this title.

Every effort has been made to contact copyright holders of any material reproduced in this book. Any
omissions will be rectified in subsequent printings if notice is given to the Publisher.

For more information about Heinemann Library books, or to order, please phone ++44(0)1865 888066, or
send a fax to ++44(0)1865 314091. You can visit our website at www.heinemann.co.uk.

Any words appearing in the text in bold, **like this**, are explained in the Glossary.

Contents

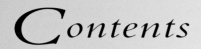

The Nazi regime

Auschwitz was one of many **prison camps** set up by the **Nazis** during the Second World War. People imprisoned here died from starvation, overwork and ill-treatment. Many more were simply sent here to be killed. People visit Auschwitz today to remember those who died. But why did the Nazis set up camps like this?

Division and persecution

In 1933 the Nazi Party, led by Adolf Hitler, came to power in Germany. The Nazis wanted Germany to be powerful. They also wanted **Aryan** people living there: blonde, blue-eyed and healthy, with 'pure' German blood. People who did not fit this image were 'undesirables'. The Nazis acted against these 'undesirables' – such as the mentally and physically disabled, black people, gypsies, homosexuals and, most of all, Jews.

The Nazis produced made-up **statistics** to blame the Jews for everything from Germany's loss of the First World War to the economic crisis in Germany. Children were taught in school that, while Germany was suffering high levels of poverty and **unemployment**, the Jews were all well off. The Nazis passed laws against Jews, stopping them from working and living where they wanted, and later depriving them of most of their other **rights**. They put their political opponents and other 'undesirables' into prison camps.

The main gate of Auschwitz I. The words across the top say: '*Arbeit Macht Frei*' (Work will set you free). It underlines the idea that the camps were set up to provide the Nazis with a pool of forced labour.

Auschwitz camp was set up in 1940, in Nazi-occupied Poland, on the site of some former Polish army **barracks**. At first it held **political prisoners**, mostly Polish. Later it was used for captured **Soviet** soldiers and Jews.

From the day it was set up until the Nazis left in 1945, the Nazis talked of Auschwitz, and the camps that grew up around it, as work camps. But the main purpose of the camps was not to provide a healthy, efficient group of workers. If so, the Nazis would have fed their prisoners more, worked them less hard and provided them with tools and equipment. The main purpose of these camps was to imprison, and later to murder, those who opposed the regime, or whom the Nazis chose to **persecute** for racial reasons, such as Jews.

There were two rows of barbed-wire fences, with **guardhouses** set all along them. Prisoners were not supposed to go near the fence. Survivors of the camp say that some guards deliberately threw prisoners' caps close to the fence and sent them to fetch the caps – knowing the prisoners would be shot for approaching the fence.

Fences and barbed wire shut off each **compound** of Auschwitz II (also called Birkenau camp) from the other compounds, the **crematoria** (in the woods at the end), the main paths and the railway line.

The barbed wire was electrified. Survivors of the camp say that many people chose to deliberately run at the fences to commit suicide. They were either shot by the guards or electrified on the fence.

How Auschwitz changed

Auschwitz was first planned to hold up to 10,000 people. Between 1940 and 1943 the camp grew and grew. The first camp, based on the Polish **barracks**, became Auschwitz I. A second, far larger camp called Auschwitz II was built nearby at Birkenau. The promise of cheap labour tempted various industries to set up factories in the area, built by prisoners from Auschwitz. By 1944 there were about 40 small camps within a few miles, providing workers for these industries. By 1944, the combined camps held hundreds of thousands of people. But millions of people had been sent there. Most died there.

In 1941 the first mass **gassing** of prisoners was held at Auschwitz – 600 **Soviet** prisoners of war and 250 patients sick with tuberculosis (an infectious lung disease). From then on more and more people were gassed. Special **gas chambers** were built to kill them in, and **crematoria** to burn their bodies. Special 'death camps' were set up, mainly for killing Jews. Birkenau became Auschwitz's death camp. At first, when a trainload of Jews reached Birkenau, selections were carried out. The old, the young and the sick were weeded out for immediate death. Strong, young men were kept to work. After 1944, selections were made less often. Everyone went straight to the gas chambers.

The main gate at Birkenau

Birkenau is much bigger than Auschwitz I. Even from the top of the main guard tower the camp stretches away as far as you can see.

6

Destroying the evidence

When the **Nazis** saw that they might lose the war, they tried to cover up exactly what had been going on in the camps, especially the death camps. In January 1945, with the Soviet army closing in on Auschwitz, the Nazis began to burn piles of official papers, blow up the gas chambers and destroy other evidence. But the Soviets advanced too quickly. The Nazis were forced to flee, herding as many prisoners as could walk to camps deeper in German territory. Many of those who were too sick to walk were shot, but there was not time to shoot them all.

The Soviets arrived at 3 pm on 27 January 1945 to find 7600 survivors in Auschwitz and its other camps. The truth about the death camps now emerged. People could see the bodies of prisoners, look at the partially destroyed records and, most importantly, they could talk to the survivors. The evidence of survivors is vital for a reconstruction of life in Auschwitz, and for an understanding of the site today. Any information that we have been given that does not come directly from the site comes from the records or survivors' stories.

A line of people, mainly women and children, are marched off to the gas chambers. Those being taken to the gas chambers were told that they were going to have a shower after their long journey. The picture above shows the site today.

7

Hard labour

This book will, for the most part, look at living conditions in Auschwitz I and Birkenau. Many buildings remain – but these cannot show the people crammed into them. Nor can they show the daily ill-treatment by the guards; the savaging by guard dogs; the regular killing for any reason, or no reason at all. This page and the next briefly describe some parts of prisoners' lives that the site cannot show, drawn from the **testimonies** of survivors.

The execution yard. The 'death wall' at the bottom is where people were shot. The barred windows on the right are the windows of the prison block. The block on the left had shutters to stop the people in Block 10 (where medical experiments were carried out) from seeing out into the yard.

New arrivals at Auschwitz spent four weeks in '**quarantine**', supposedly to stop the newcomers bringing infections into the camp. In fact, it was to terrorize them into good behaviour. They learned that they were just a number, not a person with a name, that they had no rights at all in the eyes of the **Nazis**. They spent hours standing on **roll call** and were expected to obey various orders given in German, whether they understood the language or not. They had to learn fast – those who did not were beaten brutally, even to death.

People who survived quarantine were organized into work groups, and from then on worked from dawn to dusk, sometimes even longer. Prisoners who did the hardest outdoor work always ended the day by carrying home those who had died that day. Work groups were changed regularly. The **SS** (Schutzstaffel – the Nazi soldiers who controlled the camps) thought that a combination of the high death rate and constant shifting around would stop prisoners forming **resistance** groups. It didn't, but it did make it harder to resist, as did the Nazi practice of setting groups of prisoners against each other and making certain privileged prisoners **Blockältesters** – the officials in charge of each block.

A prison within a prison

Block 11 in Auschwitz I was the prison block. It dealt with 'crimes' by Auschwitz inmates, such as not working hard enough or trying to escape. It also punished local people, such as those who formed **resistance** groups, or tried to help the prisoners by, for example, giving them food as they went to and from the camps. Block 11 had ordinary prison cells, 'standing cells' for more severe punishment and an execution yard. Punishments included beating, death by starvation in the cells, being sent to 'penal colonies' (special work camps where prisoners were worked to death) and execution.

The only light and air for the ordinary cells came from this vent into the execution yard (below).

Standing cells measured 90 cm by 90 cm. Prisoners could only stand in them, Sometimes as many as four prisoners were crammed in. They had no light and their only air came in through the vents pictured above (which could easily become blocked by snow in winter).

Processing people

Most prisoners arrived at Auschwitz and Birkenau by rail, in cattle trucks, with about 80 people crammed in each truck. **SS** officers herded them out on to the platforms in a loud rush, to scare and confuse them. What happened next varied, depending on who the new arrivals were and where they were.

Political prisoners, arriving at Auschwitz I, would go straight to be **processed**, after unloading those who had died on the journey. At Birkenau, especially with transports of Jews, there was often a 'selection' on the platform, sorting out those fit enough to work from the old, sick and children.

Few people guessed what selection meant – they thought the fit and healthy were being chosen for harder work. In fact the old, sick and most women and children were being weeded out as useless. They were led off to their deaths. Only about 20 out of every 100 people that went through selection were selected for work and so entered the records of the camp.

The selection platform at Birkenau now, and in a photo taken by SS officials just after a train had been unloaded. The men have been separated from the women and children, the selection process happens next.

Once selected, the process of turning people from human beings into numbers began. New arrivals had to take off all their clothes and put them, along with any other possessions, into paper bags. Then all the hair was shaved off their bodies, more often than not with a blunt razor. They were sent into a huge shower room to wash – the water was often deliberately made too hot or too cold.

From names into numbers

After this, they were given their prison uniforms. Finally, a **clerk** filled in a form with their personal details and gave them a number. This number was sewn on to their uniforms, and replaced their names. From 1941 onwards, many prisoners had their numbers tattooed on their left forearm. Auschwitz was the only camp where this was done, to help keep track of people, especially the bodies – the appallingly high death rate could run to hundreds in a single day.

Until 1943 all but the Jewish prisoners, who seldom entered the records at all as they were expected to die quickly, were photographed for the records. After 1943 this did not always happen.

Some of the uniforms that the prisoners wore. Clothes and shoes were handed out regardless of whether they fitted.

Auschwitz I: barracks

In 1940 most of the **barracks** in Auschwitz I were single-storey brick buildings, with several rooms leading off a wide central corridor that was used for serving meals and assembling prisoners. Several hundred prisoners were crammed into each block, depending on the number of people in the camp. Later, another floor level was added to each barrack block. Each two-storey block could hold over 1000 prisoners. By 1943 coal-burning stoves had been built into most blocks, although they were not lit regularly.

Tadeusz Iwaskzo, of the Auschwitz-Birkenau State Museum, has calculated that each prisoner had, on average, 2.5 cubic metres of sleeping space. When things became too overcrowded, even by **Nazi** standards, wooden stable-type buildings were built between the brick-built blocks. Because they were supposed to be temporary, these had no heating and only mud floors.

The difference in the colour of the bricks on this barrack block in Auschwitz I shows clearly where the second storey was added.

The prisoner in charge of the block (**Blockältester**) had his own room, and a very different level of comfort from the other prisoners. He could even collect a few possessions. But he was still a prisoner, and his position of power depended on him keeping on the right side of the **SS**.

The first prisoners at Auschwitz I slept on straw on the floor.

Later, prisoners slept on straw mattresses, packed together so tightly that they only had room to sleep on their sides.

Bunks were introduced in 1941, not for greater comfort, but so that three tiers of prisoners could be packed into a room. Depending on how full the camp was, there were at least two people to each bed.

The Blockältester's room

Living in Auschwitz I

The first prisoners in Auschwitz I had no toilets or washrooms in their **barracks**, which were just bare sleeping spaces. The whole site had just two wells of cold spring water and one large **toilet pit** outside, with a wooden bar over it to balance on.

Later, washrooms and toilets were built in each barrack block for the prisoners. There were 22 toilets to a two-storey block. The washroom had 42 taps, and sometimes soap. Prisoners could only use the toilets and washrooms at certain times (usually first thing in the morning and last thing at night). Survivors say that prisoners who spent more than a minute at the washbasin were beaten, sometimes to death.

The washrooms and toilets in a block at Auschwitz I

Food was served at the end of the corridor of each barrack block. It was cooked in the kitchen block, then taken to the barracks, in barrels or big, metal pots, by the **Blockältester**. The rations had been carefully calculated to just keep the prisoners from starving to death. By the time the **SS** officials and the prisoners in charge of the blocks had helped themselves (usually to the most nutritious things, like sausage and margarine), the 1700 **calories** prisoners were supposed to be getting had fallen to 1300 or less.

A day's ration – at best

Breakfast 500 ml of coffee or tea. This was often nothing more than dried leaves or bark, usually birch, in hot water.

Midday 750 ml of thin turnip and potato soup, sometimes with other vegetables, a scrap of meat or 'Avo' (a yeast extract) added.

Evening 300 g of bread, 25 g of margarine, 25 g of sausage or cheese and a teaspoon of beet jam.

The kitchen block of Auschwitz I. This provided food for the whole camp. By the time the food arrived at each block it was often cold. Prisoners who worked in the kitchen often took small amounts of food and fed them to people in the hospital blocks or to others who were close to death through starvation.

Birkenau BII: wooden huts

The wooden huts in Birkenau BII were originally designed as stables. You can still see the rings, three to a bay, for tying up the horses. Each hut was designed to hold 54 horses. But was converted to hold at least 400 people – although up to 1000 were often crammed in. The prisoners in charge of the hut had the two bays nearest the door. The two bays at the other end had toilet holes dug in them.

Each remaining bay had four sets of three-tiered bunks, or three sleeping shelves, one above the other, covered in paper mattresses, stuffed with wood shavings. With either arrangement there would be at least fifteen people in each bay that had been designed to hold three horses.

A wooden hut just after the liberation of the camp by the **Soviet** army in January 1945.

One of the wooden huts in Birkenau BII

Inside one of the wooden huts now – look for the rings for the horses on the crosspiece one-third of the way up the side walls.

The wooden huts in Birkenau BII had stoves at either end to keep the huts warm, although this does not mean that they were lit regularly. Even when lit, they would not have given out a great deal of heat. The smoke from these stoves was carried along the brick **flues** that ran down the middle of the hut, to the chimney at the opposite end.

Holes were made in the flues at regular intervals to allow some warmth to escape. This also meant that smoke escaped into the hut as well.

Health and hygiene

People in Birkenau BII used open **toilet pits** when the huts were first built. Then communal toilet and shower huts were built. The use of the toilets was restricted, as in Auschwitz I, usually to first thing in the morning and last thing at night for a very short time. There was no toilet paper, nor were there any hand-washing facilities. As many people had diarrhoea from **undernourishment**, these **unhygienic** conditions made matters worse.

Keeping clean

Washing was a real problem. Birkenau was on damp, marshy ground, but there was very little fresh water, and washing facilities were almost non-existent. People were not often allowed to use the showers that had been built. When they did, a whole block had to shower at the same time. They had to take off their clothes at their **barracks** and then run, naked (even in deep winter snow), to the shower block. This could be the last straw for the sick – it could kill them.

A toilet block in the wooden hut section of Birkenau. There were three rows of seats, with about 130 holes to each row.

Each **compound** of Birkenau BII had its own kitchen; the only building with fresh running water. The food was cooked here and then taken to each hut and distributed there by the **Blockältester**. Rations were the same as those in Auschwitz I, which are listed on page 15.

Prisoners at Auschwitz were badly undernourished, in many cases starving to death. This meant they had almost constant diarrhoea, pus-filled boils and were often feverish. What happened when they caught other infections, or hurt themselves while working? There were doctors among the prisoners who tried to help as much as they could. It was important for the prisoners to stay as healthy as possible, so that they looked capable of work. If they were seriously ill or injured they would either be sent to the **gas chambers** to be killed (selections were held regularly to weed out the sick) or taken to the hospital block. More often than not they were not treated in the hospital block, but used for various medical experiments.

The kitchen blocks for each section of Birkenau BII were at the same end of each compound. Now only some of the brick chimneys remain.

Birkenau BI: brick huts

The brick huts in Birkenau BI were put up quickly, with no foundations. At first the floors were just mud; later some were given concrete or brick floors. There were two stoves with a shared chimney for each side of the hut; but they were seldom lit. There were seventeen windows, which were barred shut on the outside, and two vents in the roof which were the only way to air the huts: the doors had to be shut all the time.

Prisoners slept on sleeping shelves. Sometimes they were given straw to put between themselves and the bare planks. At least four people were expected to sleep on each shelf. When a new transport arrived, the huts became more crowded – up to fifteen people were fitted on to a single shelf; enough weight, even at starvation rations, to break the planks.

One of the brick huts in Birkenau BI

The sleeping shelves of the brick huts

PLAN: Birkenau, brick huts

.·↗ doorways, with direction of opening

☐ sleeping space, three tiers, shelves

☐ Blockältester's room and bread store

▪ stoves   ☐ sinks

◖◗ toilets   ▭ windows

building height 5.80 m
building length 36.25 m
building width 11.40 m

Stoves were built at each point marked with a purple square on the plan.

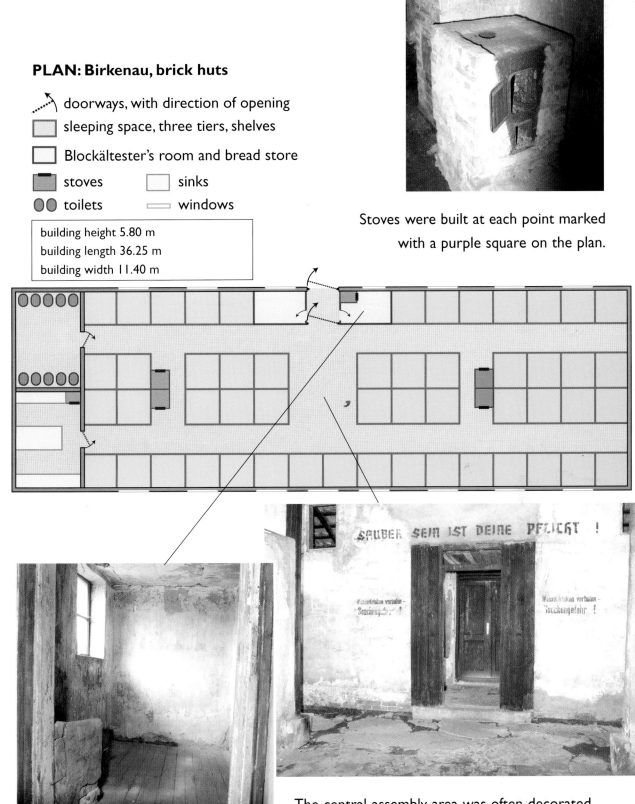

The **Blockältester** had his own room, with a stove, by the entrance.

The central assembly area was often decorated with slogans. The big sign over the door says: 'Cleanliness is your duty!' The smaller signs on each side of the door say: 'Don't drink the water, it carries contagious disease!'

Keeping clean

Although Birkenau BI had brick-built kitchens, toilets, washrooms and shower blocks, the food was the same as in other parts of Auschwitz. The showers were used as infrequently as those in BII. The use of washing facilities was also as restricted as in the rest of the camp.

Prisoners in all parts of Auschwitz were infested with fleas and lice, which could spread easily around the incredibly cramped sleeping areas. Their clothes were disinfected from time to time, and they were too – dunked in tubs full of water with chemicals such as **chlorine** added. If they refused to go right under the water, which often burned their eyes and throats just from inhaling the vapour, they were pushed under and held under, sometimes until they drowned.

The kitchen block for a BI **compound**

The shower block for a BI compound. Prisoners were herded into the showers naked, as in BII.

The washroom of a BI compound. There are places for the soap, but soap was not always available, and when it was it was a mixture of fat and ash that did not foam properly, so was hard to wash with.

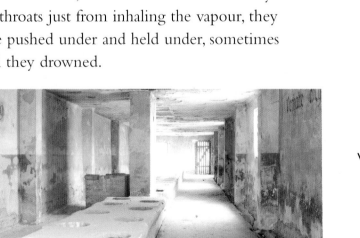

The toilets of a BI compound. They originally had stone lids, held on with a wire hook, and bars to stop prisoners trying to escape through the sewers.

Misleading impressions

Many of the huts in Birkenau BI had their own washrooms and toilets at one end of the hut, in two facing sleeping spaces. Each of these was shut off from the rest of the hut by a door and the washroom had its own stove. Each toilet block had eight china toilets, as used in Auschwitz I. Although this does not seem a lot for 700 or more people, it still seems like an attempt on the part of the **Nazis** to make living conditions more bearable.

In fact, work on the washrooms and toilets did not begin until mid 1944. Rather than a genuine attempt to make life better for the prisoners, this looks like an attempt to cover up how bad conditions had been. The washrooms and toilets were never connected to the water, drains or sewers; so they were never used. All they did was cut down the amount of room for sleeping by taking away eight shelves.

The washrooms and toilets that were never used.

Invisible people

So far, we have dealt with living in Auschwitz. From 1942 onwards more and more trainloads of people passed through Auschwitz without being recorded – straight to their deaths. They were mainly Jewish people. As the German army took over more countries, Jews from those countries were loaded on to transports for Auschwitz-Birkenau.

Their journey could take many days, all without food or water, and with just one small bucket (or nothing) to use as a toilet. Many people died on the journey. Those who survived to get off the trains at Birkenau could pass through the camp to their deaths in a matter of hours, leaving no trace behind them except the growing piles of their possessions, which filled 30 huts in a special **compound** in Birkenau BII. These possessions, ranging from clothes and hairbrushes to the shaven hair of prisoners, were kept for reuse. The **Nazis** became obsessed with getting as much profit out of their prisoners as possible.

The huge mound of suitcases in the Auschwitz State Museum shows that the people who owned them came from all over the world. Just this small part of the pile shows that people came from countries as far apart as Holland and Greece.

The Nazis blew up the crematoria at Auschwitz, where they burned the bodies of their victims, as soon as they realized the **Soviets** were advancing on the camp. They did not do a good enough job of destruction, there is still enough left to work out what the buildings were used for. The metal tracks you can see were for the carts used to slide the bodies into the ovens.

Crematorium I at Auschwitz I has been reconstructed so that visitors can see what would have happened there.

The **gas chamber** (below). Victims were told this was a shower room, where they would be able to wash after their long journey.

The rear of the crematorium (above)

The walls were thick, so were the doors, and there was a strong system of locks.

The dead were loaded, several at a time, on to carts, wheeled to the ovens and burned (below).

Zyklon B crystals (which produced a deadly gas) were poured into the room through holes in the roof.

How many people?

How many people went straight to their deaths? The simple answer is that we do not know, not even to the nearest 1,000,000 people. The latest research suggests that at least 1,500,000 unregistered people, most of them Jewish, were killed at Auschwitz. Some historians have estimated the number at closer to 4,000,000.

The **Nazis** evacuated Auschwitz in a hurry. They blew up the **crematoria** at Birkenau and set light to the huts filled with the possessions of those they had murdered. They began to burn their records too, at Birkenau and Auschwitz I. But they did not have time to completely destroy the evidence. The camps were too big and the **Soviet** army arrived sooner than expected. So there is some evidence left. This evidence, and the **testimonies** of survivors, go some way to showing the extent of the crime that was committed at Auschwitz.

Some of the millions of Zyklon B canisters found at Birkenau. The contents of these canisters were used in the **gas chambers** of Auschwitz.

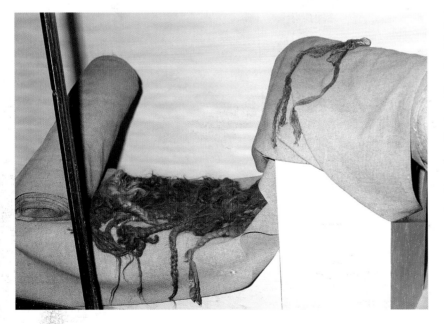

Just one of the many bolts of cloth that were scientifically analysed and found to have been made from human hair, probably female hair. About seven tonnes of hair was found when the camp was liberated, ready to be sold to make cloth or stuff mattresses.

Evidence of the crime

The Auschwitz State Museum has huge piles of belongings that were not burned by the time the Soviet army arrived. These, just a small part of the possessions put into store, show that the Nazis killed young and old, male and female. Auschwitz was one of many camps. The site brings home to us the huge scale of the Nazi operations. The belongings remind us that each one of those millions of people was not a number or a statistic, but a person, just like us.

Timeline

1933	(Jan) **Nazi** party comes to power. Hitler becomes Chancellor of Germany.
1935	Racist Nuremberg Laws passed in Germany. These discriminate against Jews, for example by forbidding marriages between Jews and non-Jews.
1939	(3 Sep) Britain and France declare war after Germany invades Poland. Start of Second World War.
1940	Auschwitz I set up
1941	Birkenau set up. A decision is made to set up death camps for the killing of Jews. (Sep) First mass **gassings** take place at Auschwitz I. (11 Nov) Germany invades USSR.
1945	(Jan) **Soviet** army nears Auschwitz. **SS** begin to destroy **crematoria** and other evidence of mass murder. (18 Jan) Auschwitz liberated by Soviet army.

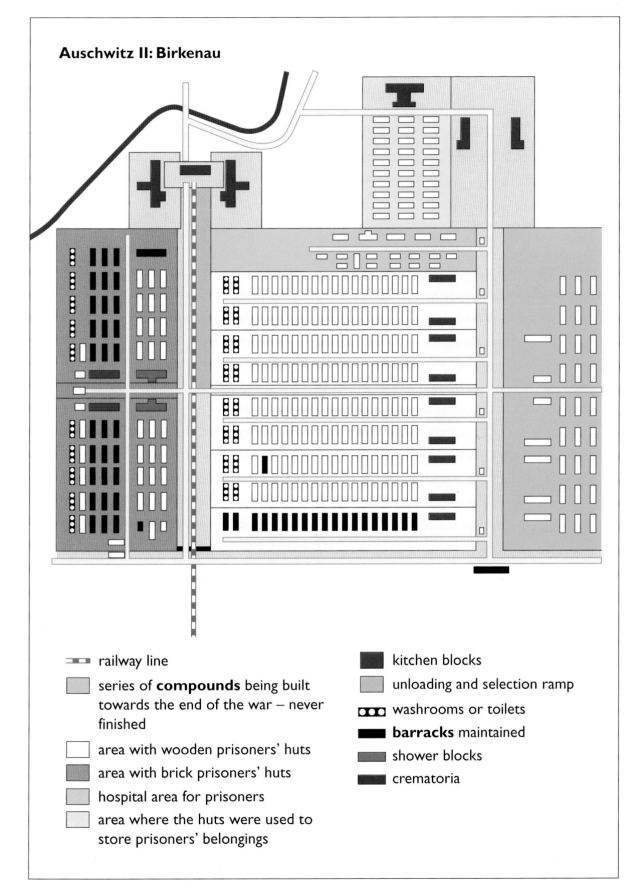

Auschwitz II: Birkenau

railway line

series of **compounds** being built towards the end of the war – never finished

area with wooden prisoners' huts

area with brick prisoners' huts

hospital area for prisoners

area where the huts were used to store prisoners' belongings

kitchen blocks

unloading and selection ramp

washrooms or toilets

barracks maintained

shower blocks

crematoria

Glossary

Aryan those whom the Nazis believed belonged to the German 'master race'. Their characteristics were said to include blonde hair and blue eyes.

barracks large buildings used to house groups of soldiers

Blockältester prisoner in charge of a block or barrack at Auschwitz. This person had to report to an SS officer.

calorie unit used to measure the energy value of food

chlorine gas which, when added to water, produces a solution which bleaches things and, if it is a strong solution, can burn the skin

clerk official record-keeper. Many of the clerks at Auschwitz were chosen from among the prisoners.

compound area containing buildings surrounded by a fence or wall

crematorium place where human bodies are burned

flue channel for carrying heat from a stove or fire

gas chamber large, well-sealed room, with access for gas or gas-producing crystals, where many people could be gassed at once. Many of these were made to look like large, communal shower rooms, to get people to go into them without resisting.

gassing killing people by exposing them to a gas which fills their lungs and stops them breathing

guardhouses places where guards can stand and watch over various parts of a protected place

Nazi member of the National Socialist German Workers' Party, which was led by Adolf Hitler and held power in Germany between 1933 and 1945

persecute treat someone cruelly or unfairly

political prisoner person imprisoned for opposing the government, usually for holding different political beliefs

prison camp camp created by the Nazis for the imprisonment of 'undesirables' such as communists, homosexuals or Jews. Many were created in Germany before the outbreak of the Second World War in 1939. Their regime was based on harsh conditions, hard labour and starvation of prisoners. After the outbreak of war, many camps were created outside Germany, particularly in Poland. Later in the war, many of these camps became 'death camps', dedicated to the extermination of prisoners, especially Jews in what became known as the 'Final Solution'.

processed having a series of things done which change and make a thing or person fit a pattern

quarantine period of isolation for newcomers to a place, to check that they do not have any infectious diseases that they could give to the people already there

resistance fighting back against an invader. The Nazis faced many resistance groups in the countries they invaded during the Second World War.

rights all people have the right to certain things, for example the right to live and the right to sufficient food and shelter. People also have different rights given to them by the laws of different countries.

roll call calling out a list of names to find out who is present

Soviet belonging to the USSR, a communist state that included Russia and many smaller nations

SS (Schutzstaffel) Hitler's personal guard, who were also responsible for overseeing the 'death camps'

statistics facts and figures

testimony any statement or evidence, such as that given in a court of law or by survivors of Nazi death camps

toilet pit hole dug in the ground, usually outside, to use as a toilet

undernourishment not having enough food to keep the body healthy

unemployment not having work

unhygienic not clean and healthy

Index